JOHNSBURG PUBLIC LIBRARY

W9-BIQ-181

Johnsburg Public Library
3000 N. Johnsburg Road
Johnsburg, Illinois 60051
815-344-0077
www.johnsburglibrary.org

NICKELS

BY MADDIE SPALDING

The Child's World®
childsworld.com

Published by The Child's World®
1980 Lookout Drive • Mankato, MN 56003-1705
800-599-READ • www.childsworld.com

Photographs ©: iStockphoto, cover, 1, 5 (top right), 5 (top left),
5 (bottom) 6, 7, 15, (top), 19, 20 (bottom); Henryk Sadura/
Shutterstock Images, 9; Shelly Greer/Thinkstock, 10, 20 (top);
Everett Historical/Shutterstock Images, 13; Shutterstock Images,
15 (bottom); Frank L. Junior/Shutterstock Images, 16–17; Shane
Maritch/Shutterstock Images, 20 (middle); Red Line Editorial, 22

Design Elements: Ben Hodosi/Shutterstock Images

Copyright © 2018 by The Child's World®
All rights reserved. No part of this book may be reproduced or
utilized in any form or by any means without written permission
from the publisher.

ISBN 9781503820029
LCCN 2016960497

Printed in the United States of America
PA02336

ABOUT THE AUTHOR

Maddie Spalding writes and
edits children's books. She lives in
Minnesota.

TABLE OF CONTENTS

CHAPTER ONE

WHAT IS A NICKEL?

Nickels are U.S. coins. They are worth five cents. One nickel can be written 5¢ or $0.05. Five pennies make one nickel. Twenty nickels make one dollar.

Two nickels make one dime.

Thomas Jefferson

When the coin was made

Thomas Jefferson is on the front of the nickel.

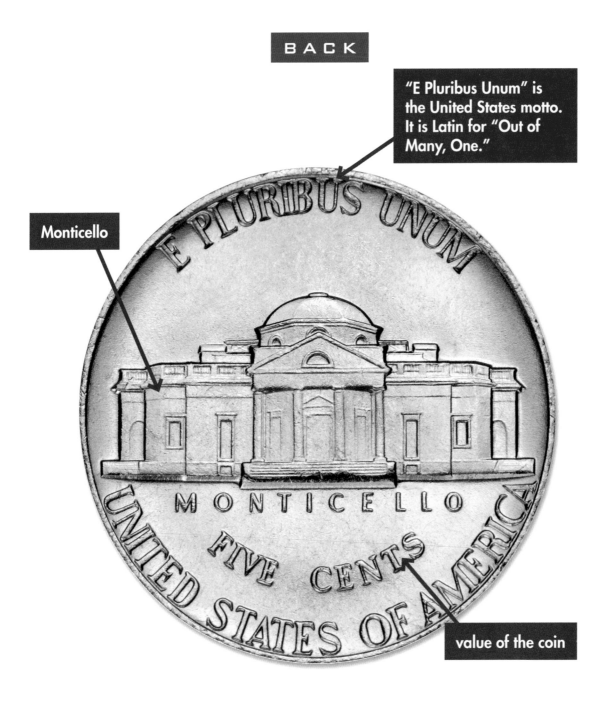

"E Pluribus Unum" is the United States motto. It is Latin for "Out of Many, One."

Monticello

value of the coin

Jefferson's house is on the back. His house is called Monticello.

CHAPTER TWO

THE HISTORY OF THE NICKEL

The United States Mint makes money. The U.S. Mint is part of the U.S. government. The first U.S. five-cent coins were **minted** in 1792. They were made from silver.

How is a nickel different from a dollar bill?

One United States Mint location is in Denver, Colorado.

Lady Liberty was on the front of the U.S. nickel in 1912.

The U.S. Mint stopped making silver five-cent coins in 1873. A new five-cent coin was made in 1866. It was called a nickel.

The nickel **design** changed many times. Thomas Jefferson was put on the nickel in 1938. President Franklin Delano Roosevelt wanted to **honor** him.

Why might Franklin D. Roosevelt have wanted to honor Thomas Jefferson?

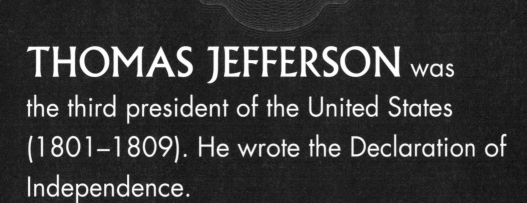

THOMAS JEFFERSON was

the third president of the United States
(1801–1809). He wrote the Declaration of
Independence.

CHAPTER THREE

MAKING A NICKEL

Nickels are made from nickel and copper. Nickel and copper are metals.

Nickel and copper metals are used to make coins.

Nickels are made of 75 percent copper.

At the U.S. Mint,
machines cut metal
into **discs**. A coin press
stamps designs on
the discs.

The U.S. Mint sends nickels to banks. Nickels travel all over the country. Each nickel has its own history.

Why do you think the U.S. Mint has six locations throughout the United States?

Coins travel around the United States.

1912 U.S. nickel

1792 The U.S. Mint made the first five-cent coins out of silver.

1866 The U.S. Mint made new five-cent coins out of copper and nickel. They were called nickels.

A U.S. Buffalo Nickel

1913 An image of a buffalo was put on the back of the nickel.

1974 U.S. nickel

1938 Thomas Jefferson first appeared on the nickel.

★ The 1792 five-cent coins were the first coins minted in the United States.

★ According to the U.S. Mint, the first five-cent coins may have been made from George and Martha Washington's melted silverware.

★ The U.S. Mint made nickels with silver from 1942 to 1945. The U.S. Navy needed nickel to make ships during World War II.

★ The U.S. Mint makes more than one billion nickels each year.

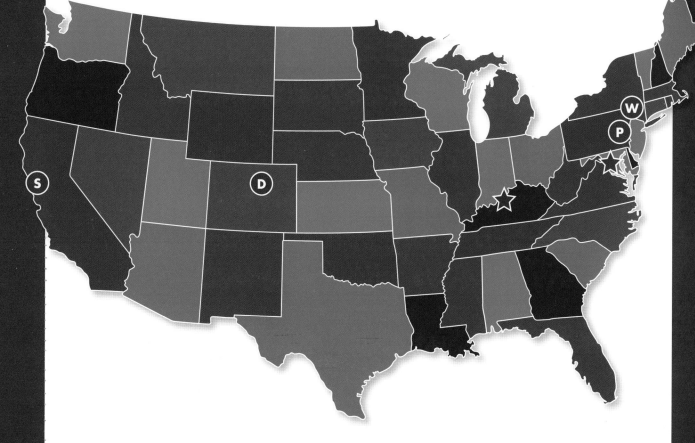

KEY

★ Fort Knox, Kentucky—Storage of U.S. gold

★ Washington, DC—Headquarters of the U.S. Mint

COIN-PRODUCING MINTS

Ⓓ Denver, Colorado—Produces coins marked with a D.

Ⓟ Philadelphia, Pennsylvania—Produces coins marked with a P.

Ⓢ San Francisco, California—Produces coins marked with an S.

Ⓦ West Point, New York—Produces coins marked with a W.

design (di-ZINE): A design is the shape or style of something. The U.S. nickel design has changed many times.

discs (DISKS): Discs are flat, circular objects. Metal is cut into discs to make coins.

honor (AHN-ur): To honor is to give praise or respect. President Franklin D. Roosevelt wanted to honor Thomas Jefferson by putting him on the nickel.

minted (MINT-ed): A coin that is minted is made out of metal. The first U.S. five-cent coins were minted in 1792.

IN THE LIBRARY

Adler, David. *Money Madness*. New York, NY:
Holiday House, 2009.

Dowdy, Penny. *Money*. New York, NY: Crabtree, 2009.

Morgan, Elizabeth. *Nickels!* New York, NY: PowerKids, 2016.

Uhl, Xina M. *Thomas Jefferson*. Mankato, MN:
The Child's World, 2017.

ON THE WEB

Visit our Web site for links about nickels: **childsworld.com/links**

Note to Parents, Teachers, and Librarians: We routinely verify our Web links to make sure they are safe and active sites. So encourage your readers to check them out!

INDEX